Afghanistan

'ROM

RY

OF

ER

Afghanistan

Roland and Sabrina Michaud

Thames and Hudson

Translated from the French by June P. Wilson

First published in Great Britain in 1980
by Thames and Hudson Ltd, London
First paperback edition 1985

Printed in Switzerland

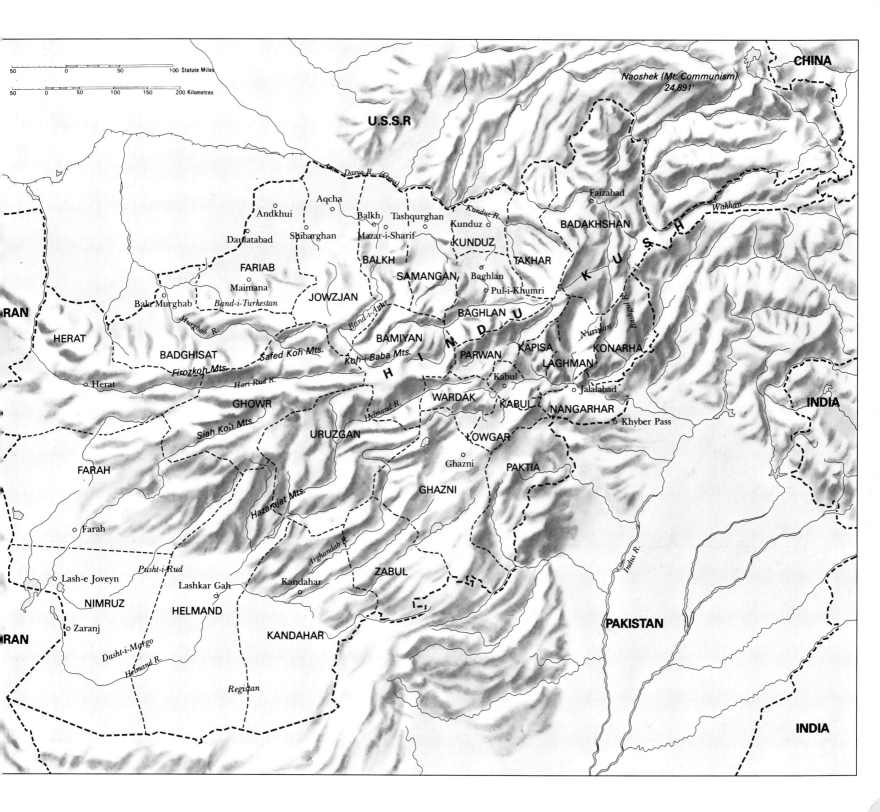

Afghanistan lies across the legendary land route from the Mediterranean to India and shares a border with Iran on the west, the Soviet Union on the north, and Pakistan on the east and south, while in the northeast it touches China's Sinkiang Province and Kashmir. This remote and strategically placed region has often proved irresistible to aggressors—Genghis Khan and Tamerlane among them—but in the past it enjoyed the protection offered by the great Hindu Kush mountain range as well as by the sturdiness and courage of its inhabitants. No natural barrier, however, could hold back the arsenal of modern weaponry unleashed by the Soviet forces on December 24, 1979, when Afghanistan was invaded and thrust into the forefront of superpower confrontation. With inexorable swiftness, the old Afghanistan was shattered, to the outrage of the entire civilized world.

Veteran travelers and photographers, Roland and Sabrina Michaud spent fourteen years, through 1979, in Afghanistan, recording a way of life—age-old, classic Islam—that most likely no longer exists. This makes the stunningly beautiful pages that follow all the more poignant, for in them we see with glowing clarity the pride, enduring faith, and self-sufficiency of a yet unconquered people. To them this book is dedicated.

The Publishers

Herat
Turquoise Oasis

Plates 1–16

To the traveler coming from the West, Afghanistan is first Khorassan, the country of the rising sun and an extension of the Iranian plateau. In the gray waste of the infinite steppes, Herat suddenly emerges like a jewel—a wide fertile valley watered by the Hari Rud. In the midst of fields and orchards crisscrossed by irrigation canals stand towers of beaten earth pierced with large holes designed to catch pigeon droppings. Peasants in white turbans cultivate barley and wheat, cumin and saffron. In the soft autumn light, the trees vibrate with color: golden planes, emerald poplars with their bright yellow tips, mulberry trees whose dried fruit— white or black—feeds the poor. It is the season for grapes, the best in the world. They flourish in seventeen varieties, of which "the bride's little finger," with its transparent, elongated seeds, is the sweetest.

When mule drivers reach the point where the path turns into an alley of dark pines, they know they have arrived at Herat. This city of beaten earth enclosed in an area a mile and a half square is divided by two perpendicular streets that carve the city into four sections. Dominated by a citadel built of dried mud, Herat is the eternal city risen seven times from its ruins. Mosques, Turkish baths, bazaars, caravansarai, and mausolea testify to its vitality. At the base of six truncated minarets, a dome coated with enamel bluer than the sky resembles an exotic fruit bursting from an excess of sugar. The city may be only earth and mud, yet it conveys a sense of grace and courtesy. Men speaking a Persian from the Middle Ages greet each other, hand over the heart. In the yellow dust raised by the jingling *gadis* decorated with red pompoms, the smells of a distant Orient stir memories of the invasions, tyrannies, carnage, and resurrections that have marked Afghanistan's history. Intellectual and artistic capital of the country, Herat is justly proud of its Great Friday Mosque and the city's patron saint, Khwaja Abdallah Ansari (1006–88).

By the 10th century, the great mosque had already begun to attract scholars and philosophers from all over the Islamic world. Today it is being lovingly restored with funds raised by a special tax on sugar. Thanks to these efforts, the structure gradually reassumes something of its ancient splendor.

It was in this mosque that young Abdallah Ansari lived among the saints and doctors of law, his reputation continuing to grow until his death at the age of 82. His tomb at Gazargah, 3 miles from the city, is much frequented by pilgrims. Surrounded by gardens, pavilions, a reservoir, cemetery, guest house, and mosque, this complex shelters a religious order made up of the saint's descendants who devote their lives to meditation and the dissemination of the master's teachings. It functions as an asylum as well, providing, in the medieval sense, a safe haven for the criminal seeking refuge from the law.

As winter arrives, a dream city emerges mantled in snow. In the biting cold, families gather under their *sandali*, a low table covered with an eiderdown, and stretch their legs against a *brasero* that gives out a comforting warmth. They eat bread with a thick grape syrup, and drink hot black tea. Colds and coughs are treated with infusions made from quince seeds.

When the snow melts, streets become a quagmire. Herati are so bespattered by passing *gadis* that they fill the public baths. Finally spring comes. Migrating birds form wheeling clouds in the sky; children fly their kites. On Friday (the Islamic day of rest) families take picnics to the *ziarats*—the tombs of the saints—and feast on grape cheese.

In the gardens, pomegranate petals fall like snowflakes. Rich Heratis repaint their brass-studded doors the color of paradise. Behind these doors, they live out their idea of paradise in a closed world of simplicity and serenity. In teahouses, the men sniff pink roses and smile as they watch their wives go by, swathed from head to foot in their pleated *chadri* whose colors repeat the ocher, mauve, and blue-gray of the hills. Women see the world filtered through the embroidered *musharabieh* that cover their faces. The Koran says: "They will have beautiful women with large black eyes, women beautiful like carefully hidden pearls." They are veiled the better to make men dream.

Then comes summer. From June to September, the wind has the sound of the sea and causes the pine trees to moan. Coming from Nimruz, it turns the city into an ocean of swirling dust. Yet without it life would be hell. It blows away insects and epidemics, and tempers the terrible heat. Heratis eat salted cucumbers sometimes mixed with yogurt diluted with water, drink green tea and take long siestas. Thus, the cycle begins again.

Nimruz
Pirates and Ruins in the Desert

Plates 17–27

In Zaranj, the capital of Nimruz, Sufi Djan offers us his hospitality. He comes from a long line of large landowners. His food is refined, his garden full of flowers, the temperature mild even though it is winter. "You cannot imagine the care it takes to keep these flowers alive!" he says, as if reading my thoughts. "Ours is a thirsty soil, and every drop of water is as precious as diamonds. So precious in fact that when a man stole water, he used to be condemned to death where an ordinary thief had only his hand cut off. This soil is burned by the sun, swept by the wind, deprived of water and shade. Man must fight incessantly to scratch a bare sustenance from it."

Yet the Hindu Kush has blessed this desert with the waters of the Helmand, a powerful river that manages to provide a little arable land, a little life to the arid soil. As it flows its thousand miles, the Helmand divides the vast, low-lying region into two parts. From the river's right bank north stretches Dasht-i-Margo ("Desert of Death"); on its left and south, Registan ("Land of Sands"). Finally, after a bend in its course, the Helmand is diverted into a series of lagoons.

With only two seasons, Nimruz is brutalized by variations in temperature. From April to November, it is a furnace; from December to March, the temperature can drop to −20° C. Whichever the season, the climate's chief characteristic is wind. Although this can reach a force of 120 miles an hour, its benefits outweigh all inconveniences. In summer, the wind cools the houses as it blows through screens laced with dampened thornbushes that cover doors and windows.

Suffocating heat, insufficient rainfall, and thick incrustations of salt have rendered most of the land sterile. "Yet," Sufi Djan continues, "wherever you can introduce water, the soil is very fertile. Our ancestors mastered the science of irrigation and the art of gardening." His ancestors were the Tajiks, now called Farsiwan because all the nonnomadic peoples, like their Iranian neighbors in Khorassan, speak Persian. Peace-loving farmers and merchants, the Tajiks believed in law and order. Near the dawn of civilization, they produced engineers of uncommon talent who were able to conceive and execute a vast network of irrigation canals. Subterranean conduits brought water to agrarian centers. One canal, 35 miles long, connected the city of Shar-e-Gholghola with a dam on the Helmand.

To reach fortified Nimruz, the traveler drives over gray rubble, zigzagging through a labyrinth of crescent-shaped dunes over 100 feet high. It was the wind that made these great ridges, resembling a succession of surging waves frozen in midmotion. But their immobility is only an illusion, for the wind moves them 10 inches a day. Called *barkane*, or "marchers," by the Nimruz, the dunes have great destructive power, swallowing roads, ruins, and anything else that stands in their way. Shar-e-Gholghola is a city risen from the sand. Impressive remains bear witness to the great empires long since gone, making a macabre boneyard that still haunts men's memories.

Positioned at the junction of three frontiers and between the ancient civilizations of Mesopotamia and the Indus, Nimruz has played an important role in human history. As the cradle of the Aryan world, it has shared life with Persian, Greek, and Arab conquerors. In the end it was the Arabs who gave the city its identity, doing so by imposing Sunnite Islam.

Tradition claims that the 13th-century hordes of Genghis Khan and those of Tamerlane 150 years later destroyed the waterworks and burned or killed all that impeded their progress. This is only partly true. More important was a change in climate, which made it impossible for the soil to support both the Tajiks and the tribute demanded of them by the nomads. Most of these migrated, some integrating with the Baluch on the banks of the Helmand, some with the Brahui in Registan.

During the summer, the Helmand winds through sand and gravel, but clumps of tamarisk and reeds are the only evidence of its passage. Sufi Djan says: "The river is our only hope of life, but with its floods, it destroys as much as it generates."

This may be why the Baluch spend only part of each year in their small villages on the riverbanks. During the winter, they cultivate the meager plots that hug each side of the channel. But by the end of spring, they have abandoned their villages and set up camp at the base of the mountains.

The British once called these people "their bravest enemy" in Asia. Valiant fighters though they were, the Baluch proved no match for the Pathans, Nimruz' most recent conquerors. Constant shifts still make the Baluch hard to capture, but they remain vulnerable to the Pathans' feudal ways of appropriating land and flocks unless the vassals pay tribute money. This collection of taxes involves a constant struggle between superior force and cunning.

For a long time, the Baluch were also pillagers and mercenaries. Today they are professional smugglers carrying on a brisk trade between Afghanistan, which produces the world's best opium, and Iran, the drug's largest consumer.

But the real desert men are the Brahui. A powerful desire for independence led these people to settle in the middle of Registan. With the moving sands on one side and Pakistan's abrupt mountain ranges on the other, their liberty would seem assured. A fierce tribe, they submit to no law except the law of retaliation. If they survive infancy, their resistance grows with the hard life they have to endure. Indifferent to privation, they can stand extreme fatigue and long and arduous marches under the hottest sun without food or water. Their centuries-old experience at digging wells deeper than the height of a minaret has made it possible to exist in this desolate wasteland. Life is organized around the 15 or so wells dug as much as 45 miles apart. Flocks of goats and sheep radiate away from these water holes, returning to drink only every three days.   Shepherds must abide   by this rule at the risk of losing their flocks or watching them die of thirst.

Shepherds and flocks spend their days on the move searching for food. Although scant, fodder has a high nutritive value due to the lack of rain, which helps preserve mineral riches drawn from the soil. At nightfall, man and beast gather around a fire lighted with *saxaul*, a silvery-gray and white tree without leaves, and maintained with sheep droppings.

When a traveler arrives at a Brahui camp, he kisses the Khan's hands and is embraced in turn. Thereafter follows a quarter-hour of greetings and news—good news only, no matter what the tribulations recently undergone. The visitor is then offered a seat, and tea is served immediately. The first cup must be very sweet, which does little to slacken the thirst. Then, slowly and with every word measured, conversation begins, punctuated with sips of increasingly bitter tea. Each syllable and gesture is savored, but the look counts for even more. The smoke of the water pipe that travels from hand to hand leaves ideas hanging in suspension. Life winds down in the camp between the high dunes.

Another time, the traveler was greeted with a scene out of the Bible. As a patriarch crippled with rheumatism crumbled bread with gnarled hands and fed it to some baby lambs, ragged children in caps emblazoned with gold and multicolored threads drew near, like flies attracted to honey. The old man's eyes had an expression of extraordinary purity. "Father," I asked him, "are you the desert's only smile?" "The desert has unpredictable ways," he said. "You don't know its smile. In the spring, after the rains, it is covered with a thousand flowers—a thousand smiles. The least thornbush becomes a celebration in buds and blossoms. It is easier to transform the desert into rich pastures than it is to change a man."

Bazaars of Central Asia

Plates 28—42

The era when caravans of several hundred camels laden with Asia's most exotic merchandise wended their way from India to Bokhara, by way of Kabul, and from Persia to China, by way of Herat, has come to an end. Trade in indigo, brocades, silks, and spices has disappeared, and commerce in tea, grains, fruit, and leather continues only at the rate of a trickle. Yet, away from the macadam roads, the unhurried traveler can still catch a glimpse of the eternal Orient in the small forgotten towns where caravans used to stop, towns where memories of *A Thousand and One Nights* still linger. In their tiny shops, merchants sit cross-legged on cushions, their eyes fastened on every passerby. All the ethnic strains of Central Asia rub shoulders in the bazaars.

Look and listen closely, for the bazaars are the repositories of traditions a millennium old. Only by frequent and diligent visits to the markets can the foreigner learn the secrets of Afghan life.

First comes courtesy: "Peace be with you! Are you well? How are things going with you? Are you really well? You look well! You seem to be doing well! You're not feeling tired? Be of good cheer!" These phrases follow each other like the telling of rosary beads, and the recipient must answer in kind, although perhaps with greater speed.

Then there is the tradition of hospitality. A merchant must serve tea to all visitors, whether they buy anything or not. He dispatches his assistant to the nearest teahouse—often called *samawat* after the Russians' samovar—to fetch hot water. The teahouse has two brass samovars, one heating while the other is in service. Today, porcelain teapots and cups are being replaced by aluminum pots and plastic glasses. Gradually, the bazaars of Afghanistan evolve into flea markets, and Ali Baba's cave is fast becoming a suburban supermarket.

Yet the tradition of honesty remains. The Koran is unequivocal: "And the Sky devised scales so that you may not cheat. Give true weight and never tamper with the scales." In a country where only recently a thief was nailed by his ear to his victim's house, weighing remains a solemn affair. Holding the scales in his hand, the weigher begins the ceremony with a prayer calling for a divine benediction to oversee the operation. Then he waits until the two pans are in balance and recites a formula that helps him remember the number of previous weighings. The operation concludes with a last benediction accompanied by the typical Moslem gesture of grasping one's beard with the right hand.

And there is the engaging subtlety attached to the tradition of generosity. Just as the merchant withholds his alms until the day's business has shown a profit, so the beggar defers the exercise of his profession until afternoon.

If you would penetrate deeper into the ways of the bazaar, you must patronize the shops. The druggist sells mysterious herbs, condiments, cosmetics, and dyes. The fruit dealer polishes his apples and pomegranates until they gleam like rubies, then piles them into perfect pyramids. In front of his modest stall, Master Kebabi grills succulent pieces of lamb on skewers over charcoal, alternating the lean meat with the fat, which the customer can season either with the juice of bitter oranges or with a powder made of dried mulberries. If you wish to know how to remove the smell of goat from your newly purchased goatskin bottle, you will be told to keep filling it with water mixed with mud and chopped straw for three days. Or do you wish a shave and a haircut? A visit to the barber is always instructive. According to an old saying: "The barber's wisdom and breadth of soul are greater than the wisest and most powerful of men, for his hand has held the heads of kings."

Tashqurghan
Partridge Fights

Partridges—*kaouk* in Persian—are very common throughout Afghanistan. The village people catch them young with nets as the birds come to the mountain springs to drink. But they are caught neither for their delectable flesh nor for the beauty of their voices. Afghans capture partridges—and males only—in order to train them for battle. Once the fowl have been caged in their handsome wicker enclosures, these are covered with a blue cloth made by the local tailor, especially colored and decorated with tie-dyed white circles and lines. The shrouds are designed to protect the birds from insect bites, dust, and cold. Then begins a rigorous training. Well nourished on wheat in winter and on the almond of apricot

Plates 43–50

pits and raisins in summer, all washed down with plenty of fresh water, the birds have their feet, wings, and beaks strengthened according to well-tested methods. For example, when evening comes and the day's work is done, the master takes his partridge to the river's edge and, keeping a steady pace, makes the bird chase after its cage baited with the evening meal. This exercise is designed to toughen the bird's feet.

Finally, it is spring. Fights are scheduled on Tuesdays and Fridays—at dawn to avoid the heat of the sun. Two days before the fight, the partridge is deprived of food and exposed to sun and dust. As its condition weakens, the fowl is ready for combat. The villagers begin to arrive, solemnly carrying their shrouded cages, the silence broken by hundreds of muffled partridge calls. They converge on the ruins of the citadel of Mallativa not far from the bazaar, there forming a large circle. Within this simplest of arenas, the combatants take each other's measure. Two umpires, one for each bird and both responsible for the conduct of the fight, enter the circle, remove the cages' coverings and the detachable bases. The birds are now alone in the arena. Immediately, they engage one other boldly, beaks pecking, wings flapping, each trying to dominate the other. The beauty of the spectacle lies in its finesse. The contestants spend long moments in feigning tactics, then do an abrupt volte-face to surprise the adversary. The spectators—only male adults and children may attend—cheer their favorites on. Bets are made between masters and those without birds. Bank notes pass from hand to hand. Meanwhile, the umpires—cages held above their heads—shadow their birds, and as soon as one of them scores a point, down comes the cage to protect the bird from harm or fatigue. Partridges never fight to the death. Once a combatant starts running away to escape his pursuer, the fight is over. The highest scorer wins.

Partridge fights are particularly popular in Tashqurghan, and bets can run very high. Fights are granted an exemption from municipal regulations, and concessionaires buy the right to levy taxes on bettors and spectators.

Municipal peccadilloes aside, the spectacle of man, bird, earth, and sky against the backdrop of Central Asia's imposing mountains is not soon forgotten.

Turkestan
The Silk Route

Plates 51–57

The Asia of the steppes is a continental sea crossed since the dawn of civilization by merchants' caravans and conquerors' armies. It could also be called a continent of dust. As a local proverb has it: "Wherever there is water and alluvium, you are sure to find a rogue." And it is from this very alluvium—the loess of the geologists—that Iranian and Turkish peasants and, at Asia's other extremity, the Chinese have established their villages, built irrigation canals, and harvested their crops. A stubborn earth in which to put down roots.

In Turkestan dust covers everything. Trees, people, and all other forms merge in the same tonality: yellow. On trails winding between high cliffs of loess, riders, mule drivers, and men on foot stir up clouds of dust the color of pepper. But come spring, lilies, variegated tulips, and other bulb flowers come into bloom. For a brief moment, the steppes are almost gaudy. The Turks call this joyous moment *eulnek*—the blossoming of the fields—which they immortalized with their invention of woven silk and threads knotted into rugs. The rug that transforms a hovel into a palace or the caftan metamorphosing the country bumpkin into a prince is like the miracle of an oasis—a butterfly pinned onto the gray expanse of the steppes. The silk route, the world's most prestigious artery, passed that way.

The secret of making silk had been jealously guarded by the Chinese for over 2,000 years. To this day, in Afghan Turkestan, silk is still woven in the traditional way. Every year, at winter's end, a representative of the Karadja Turkman tribe travels to the city of Baghlan in northeastern Afghanistan to buy the eggs of silkworms imported from Japan. These come in boxes each containing four thimbles, any one of which should produce about 15 pounds of silk. Three hundred of the boxes are brought back to the village. The Turkman women carry the eggs in a cloth tied around their necks so that the body's heat can speed the hatching of the eggs. The hatched silkworms are then placed on large platters and fed a diet of mulberry leaves, replenished several times a day. Once matured to the size of a thumb, they are transferred to flat wooden trellises covered with mulberry branches and placed in a "rearing house" under a cupola-shaped ceiling. The worms have such a prodigious appetite that it automatically limits production. About 220 pounds of mulberry leaves are required to feed enough worms to spin 25 pounds of cocoon, which in turn will produce 2 pounds of silk thread. But only half this amount can be reeled, just enough to weave one *chapan*—the striped caftan of the Turkman.

At the end of forty days of unremitting attention—to demanding creatures that do not like noise, vibration, drafts, strong smells, or pregnant women, and that refuse to eat wet mulberry leaves—the silkworm withdraws into its cocoon made of a threadlike secretion and gradually transforms itself into a chrysalis. The cocoons are put to dry in the sunshine so as to kill the chrysalis. Otherwise, the developing butterfly would pierce the cocoon and prevent it from producing a continuous strand. After this sunbath, the cocoons are thrown into boiling water, which partially dissolves the gum holding the strands together. As attendants stir the liquid bath, using paddles with little extensions that catch the end of each filament, the silk unwinds. Now several filaments or strands can be joined, depending on the thickness of the thread desired, and introduced into a reeling machine. There the thread is gently wrung to eliminate all water and wound around a large wooden wheel.

The method used in Turkestan makes it possible to dye the same thread with several colors in contiguous areas. The threads to be used in a single design are grouped together and, by selected section, tied in a tight knot. They are then plunged into a basin of dye, which colors only the parts left untied. Thus treated in a succession of knots and a variety of dye baths, one thread can have three or four colors. The design of the cloth emerges once threads of different colors have been juxtaposed. The result is a fabric of extraordinary delicacy, variety of design, and ravishingly subtle color.

The Hindu Kush
Mountains of Sand and Snow

Plates 58–66

Afghanistan, it has been said, is the land of the *Hindu Koh* ("Indian Mountains"), which, thanks to an old Persian pun, became *Hindu Kush*, or "Killer of Indians." Thus modified, the name seems a fitting memorial to all those who died of the cold in high mountain passes, prodded by Afghans toward the slave markets of Central Asia.

Even before the advent of Islam, the Hindu Kush separated the Hindu from the world of Zoroaster. This formidable barrier marks the dividing line between Central and Southern Asia and forms one of the greatest and least-known mountain ranges in the world. A stepping-stone to the Himalayas, it has long played a major role in history. Now, more than ever, this ancient region is crucial and strategic, an area where the future of the world may well be determined. Dominating the entire country, the Hindu Kush runs westward from its highest point in the Pamirs, in the adjacent Soviet Union (24,891 feet), almost to the Iranian frontier. Its principal chain extends some 700 miles and develops secondary ridges both north and south.

Actually, "Hindu Kush" refers only to the eastern and central parts of the chain. Where this joins the center of the Pamirs, the system becomes continuous with the Karakorum range, itself a western arm of the Himalayas. The Hindu Kush proper originates on the *bam-e-dunya* ("roof of the world") in the steep northeastern corner of the country, where the narrow corridor of Wakhan, variously called "panhandle" or "duck's beak," inserts a finger between the Soviet Union and Pakistan to touch China. Along a southwesterly course, it divides the vast valleys of the Amu Darya—the ancients' Oxus River—and the Indus River basin, forming a succession of mauve ridges erupting into high peaks furrowed with pockets of snow and blue glaciers. But the altitude begins to drop at the Pakistan border near the source of the Bashgul River, and continues to do so all the way to Kabul (7,820 feet). About 125 miles from the capital, it connects with the Koh-i-Baba ("Ancestral Mountains"), thus extending the watershed to the vicinity of Bamiyan in central Afghanistan. There the Hindu Kush divides into two parallel ranges, Siah Koh and Safed Koh ("Black Mountains" and "White Mountains"), and, while still losing elevation, becomes the Firozkoh ("Turquoise Mountains"). These are the "Paropamisus" of old, a corruption of Parnassus used by Aristotle in 330 B.C. in his *Meteorologica* to describe the Hindu Kush. The Paropamisus acts as a barrier between Herat, the country's principal western city, and the Soviet Union.

From every angle, the Hindu Kush is a complex and confusing terrain that fascinates but ultimately beggars description. In the easternmost regions, in the valleys of the Kunar and Nuristan, its slopes are dense with magnificent forests of cedar, pine, and larch. A little farther west, these same slopes become barren and brown, covered with a grass that is stubby yet sufficient to feed the immense herds that cross the plains between their winter quarters and summer pastures. Although this area resembles a desert, the waters from melting glaciers make some irrigation possible, and the resourceful peasants manage to grow barley and rice in fields of near-microscopic size.

During the remorseless heat of summer, a fine dust veils the landscape and blurs all outlines and contours, while the sun drains everything of color. As a result, the mountains look out of focus as if viewed through a badly adjusted lens. Images refuse to resolve, creating a jumbled and fuzzy picture suggestive of a mirage rather than reality. On the other hand, early morning and evening have a magical effect. At those hours, the countryside assumes the appearance of a Persian miniature. It becomes a world of color, shifting constantly from delicate to vibrant, picking out the vivid green of rice paddies, barley fields, orchards, and poplars, the streams edged with willows, the carpets of flowers, the peasants' clothing.

Two peasants, keeping pace with their shadows as they follow the river's edge, have just stopped to picnic off a handful of dried mulberries and a round loaf of bread, then blissfully cool their feet in the running water. In Afghanistan, where thyme and absinthe perfume the air, the notion of paradise is never far away.

Endless trails crisscross the stony, scraggly desert, their flanks strewn with the skeletons of animals. Here, a dead mule exposes its multicolored viscera to the white sky; over there, thistles gently sway on the bare sides of hills that in springtime acquire a mantle of piercing green. And when one traveler meets another, he greets him with a ritual *Manda nabashen* ("May you keep your strength"), to which the other responds *Zenda bashen* ("Long life to you").

After years spent in this country of ridges deeply etched like those on the Mongol faces of its people, the Western world seems like a place of artifice. The suffering imposed by the land has rendered the peasant pure in heart, and so he is able to submit to his difficult existence ungrudgingly. He is at one with the natural environment.

The mountains of Hazarajat in central Afghanistan, some bald yet very handsome in their contours, bearded or clean-shaven according to the season, appear to descend from the sky in an infinite succession of waves, each a different color: buff, gray, green, yellow, brown. Only the traveler crossing this wasteland gives it scale. Man remains the essential yardstick for measuring our planet's dimensions.

Wind-blown mountains clad with dust—or camelhair robes, or panther skins—grow *heng* (*asafoetida*), a gum resin that exudes from the root of a common umbelliferous plant (*Ferula foetida*) and is much prized by the Indians. So potent and long-lasting is the substance's garlicky aroma that the Sanskirt language calls it "Bactrian condiment," Bactria being the ancient name for this corner of Afghanistan. Then there are the perfect curves of the pale yellow hills that have inspired local architectural forms ideally suited to the climate, hills where nomad children collect goat and sheep droppings for the family fuel. Also the high plateaus with their savage, blinding wind, and the deep gorges so narrow that the sun never penetrates. But the mountains of Hazarajat provide valleys as well, and here is where the spirit can finally breathe.

In a house of beaten earth, the lowliest of villagers moves barefoot over his vegetable-dyed *quilim* rugs. On a hot summer afternoon, he savors the finest melons in the world, slicing through the pale green skin with a sharp knife onto a large scarlet platter. Then, stretched out on plump, flowered cushions, he dozes, a fan in his hand. At nightfall, he sits cross-legged and, by the light of a lamp lit with a cotton wick dipped in sesame oil, he reads a verse from the Koran. This is the only book he needs, the one that permits him to distinguish between the true and the false. Soon, his wife will bring him a bowl of yogurt in which he dips his bits of bread. As a Muslim, he is believed by the world at large to have several wives. Actually, he cannot afford them, nor can 98 percent of his kind.

The real man needs only that which is indispensable.

The Pathans
Frontierless Nomads

Plates 67–81

In 1893 British officers of the Indian Army established the Durand Line, an artificial border designed to protect the northwest frontier of Her Majesty's Empire. Today, on either side of this border, live twelve million Afghans called the *Pushtun* or, by the English and Indians, Pathans. They are divided into several tribes, which in turn are subdivided into larger and lesser clans. James Darmstetter, a Frenchman who translated their songs in 1888, classified the Pathans into three groups: the Afghans of the Emir, meaning the independent Emirate in Kabul; the Afghans of the Queen, or those in British India; and the Afghans of Yashestan, the diehards of the northwest frontier, a free and undisciplined, insolent, and ungovernable people. Things have changed little since, except that one hears more and more talk of an independent Pathanistan—or Pushtunistan.

Half in Afghanistan, half in Pakistan, these tough nomads and mountain people have never recognized the frontier that separates brothers and cousins, and continue to cross from one country to the other, using the numerous unpatrolled mountain trails rather than the official border posts.

The Pathans conquered Afghanistan in the 18th and 19th centuries. Overflowing the southern and southeastern parts of the country, they spread to the west, center, and north. Wherever they went, the Pathans elbowed out the indigenous people, forced them off their best lands, and generally acted like feudal barons. Now, representing the dominant ethnic group in Afghanistan, they occupy virtually every post in the government and administration. But they are also large landowners, shopkeepers, peasants, and even truck drivers. Under the monarchy some Pathan tribes were actually excused from military service. Smugglers of extraordinary impunity, the Pathans as a group have been the privileged class in every regime. The other ethnics see little merit in them, although in popular usage, only Pathans are given the designation "Afghan." It was they, after all, who created Afghanistan by establishing an independent kingdom.

A 10th-century chronicler described the Pathans thus: "Those diabolical Afghan lancers penetrated passes as a gimlet enters wood, clambered up the slopes like goats, and rushed down them like torrents." During the reign of Genghis Khan, the Pathans were probably the only adversaries to hold their own against the Conqueror of the World, dealing him his most brutal defeat. Nearer our own time, in 1843 during the first Afghan War, an army of three thousand British and local troops was exterminated, and today the Soviet invaders have bogged down in a war that may well last a long time.

The Pathans are Indo-Europeans of a tall, lean build, their color swarthy, hair sleek and black, noses strong. They wear thin mustaches, use kohl around their eyes, often wear a gold ring in one ear, and sport magnificent turbans tied to resemble cockscombs. Vests threaded with gold are worn over embroidered white shirts, trousers are very full, and sturdy boots curl up at the toes. Usually armed with a rifle and festooned with cartridges, Pathans look very dashing. They are very proud of their reputation as warriors and very quick to take offense. Their code—*Pushtunwali*— emphasizes the concept of honor, laws of asylum, hospitality, and revenge, with vendettas holding the place of greatest respect. The Pathans' 18th-century poet, Kushal Khattack, formulated this ideal in Pushtu, an Indo-European language not unlike the Dari-Persian of Afghanistan and, like it, written in Arabic letters. These are the country's two official languages, of which a proverb says: "Pushtu falls like pebbles on sand, Persian melts on the tongue like sugar."

Pathans love to sing, also to dance, in an energetic war step accompanied on a large drum called a *dhol.* Dancers twist, turn, and leap, with hair whipping against their faces. Their national sport—*naïza bazi* (called "tent-pegging" by the British)— is an excellent war game. It is also an exercise in dexterity, originally devised to train Pathan horsemen to overwhelm an encamped, sleeping enemy. By prying loose tent pegs with a three-pronged lance, the Pathans created panic.

Afghanistan has every form of nomadic life; indeed, it is the last refuge of the great nomads. The Pathans number two million nomads, and since time immemorial these have been moving their flocks from summer pasturage on the high plateaus of the Hindu Kush to winter quarters on river banks as far distant as the Indus in Pakistan. For them, transhumance is a vital necessity. The flock is the determining factor, for it must at all costs find food.

A Pathan camp set up during migration is a memorable sight. At dawn, wisps of blue smoke rise from the conglomeration of black tents resembling bats—the Persians call them leather butterflies—that hug the dun-colored hills. Around the camp slender, supple women with a wild beauty and warm laughter walk barefoot, their features masked by mysterious tatoos, heavy silver ornaments around their necks, their red dresses billowing out in the wind.

When camp is struck, the tribe starts marching slowly and inexorably through a breathtaking landscape under starry summer skies, the cavalcade accompanied by the baaing of sheep and the bleating of goats mingled with the curious roar of camels and the barking of dogs.

Nuristan
Land of Light

"There are clouds today and the panther howls in the mountains," Shukur Khan said as he brought us our breakfast. It was winter, and we were at his native village,

Plates 82–92

in one of Nuristan's valleys, having arrived there on foot after a four-day drive from Kabul to Bargomatal.

About 120 miles northeast of Kabul as the crow flies, Nuristan hugs the southern flank of the Hindu Kush. Long isolated from the rest of the country, its wild valleys are connected by mountain passes blocked by snow four and five months of the year. Summits reaching 17,000 feet frame the valleys, dotted here and there with small villages that cling to the precipitous slopes like eagles' nests.

Shukur Khan has the open face of all mountain people, whether they live in the Alps, the Carpathians, or the Caucasus, together with the black hair and beard of a Robinson Crusoe. His build is lean, his stride easy like that of a backwoodsman. The outside of his house is decorated with the magnificent horns of *markhor* (wild sheep), the highly prized trophy that bespeaks a great hunter. His eyes light up when he talks about his favorite sport, a passion Shukur Khan shares with most of his countrymen. Not only the *markhor* but also the snow panther wander about this region. In winter, however, hunger often drives wolves, fox, and bear to the outskirts of the village.

Kafiristan, or "Land of the Infidels," was the name given the area before an Afghan emir forcibly converted the population to Islam in 1895. He named it Nuristan, or "Land of Light," meaning "Light of Islam." There is a Persian proverb that describes the Pathans as "having accepted only half the Koran." If that is so, then the Nuristani have barely absorbed one-quarter. Consciously or not, they still resist Islam, and some of their rites betray lingering remnants of paganism.

Shukur Khan goes to his stables every day and returns with the little that was milked. He also brings the weaned lambs, which the women feed with leaves picked in the mountains. Shukur Khan is a rich man because he owns—in addition to cultivated fields—15 cows, a mare, her colt, and 400 goats. In ancient times, goats were sacred, and the mountain people revered them as symbols of virility. No slave could own one; only freemen.

In Nuristan, one was born either aristocrat or slave. *Bari* is the name given the slaves, a caste of artisans who by inheritance take on the lowliest trades, becoming blacksmiths, potters, cobblers, basket weavers, jewelers, masons, and wood carvers. Even though King Amamullah, who ruled from 1919 to 1929, abolished slavery, the same relationships between *bari* and lord obtain today. A subtle game of words has altered the term "lord" to mean "protector," with "slave" converted into "a protégé who owes taxes to his master." The only advantage granted the *bari* by Islam is the right to leave their localities in search of a better life elsewhere. They are especially attracted to the military, where a few have achieved high rank. But once back home, they revert to the status of slaves.

Leaving our host, we crossed the sunlit valley of the Bashgul. All around us rose jagged mountains, their slopes thick with dark pines and lightly dusted with snow. Young peasant women were on their way back from gathering wood and skipped down the mountainside, oblivious to the weight of the conical baskets strapped to their shoulders. Made of goat's wool stretched over a wooden frame, these baskets are used equally for carrying wood, grain, manure, and children. The women went barefoot, but with their legs bound in strips of cloth to protect them from brambles and brush. Ploughing and seeding are also woman's work, while the men herd sheep, considering themselves warriors. After all, they do have to defend their flocks against wild animals and thieves.

At Afsai, our second stop, two things caught our eye: one, the strategic position of the village on a hill so rugged that it was virtually inaccessible; the other, the terraces, irrigated by an ingenious system of canals and so tiny as to allow room for only two women and a spade. The flat roofs of the houses nestling one on top of the other formed giant steps up the steep slope. The village stopped just short of a ravine jutting out over the river. More torrent than river, the powerful waters turned the stones of several mills downstream. Once over the single wooden bridge, the traveler found himself at the foot of the village, as forbidding as the base of an impregnable fortress.

From Afsai, we followed a goat path to Saret. Sometimes it hugged escarpments of schist glittering with mica, or clung to cliffs that we inched along laboriously. The way could also plummet into the deep valley below. Little wonder that most of these trails were impassable to beasts of burden.

Once in Saret, we received a warm welcome from a local dignitary. He immediately took us to his veranda and served tea, accompanied by bread and honey covered with clarified butter. Below us, men danced at a wedding celebration. Shoulders hunched, they stretched out their arms like the wings of great birds of prey. In days gone by, every event of importance, from birth to death, served as an occasion for dancing. There even was dancing at sick men's bedsides in the hope of chasing away the devil to relieve their symptoms.

For us, at least, the gods of the mountains are far from dead. To paraphrase Kipling's *The Man Who Would be King:* "Come, Sahib, accompany us on the road and I will sell you a charm that will make you King of Kafiristan."

The Citadel of Islam
Madmen of God

Plates 93–98

Even if he has not been to school, the Afghan knows that all things created reflect the Creator. He knows that the secrets of the world can be summed up in a flower, and that to smell a rose is, after a fashion, to become that rose. He loves music, poetry, and games, which in no way interfere with his being a good Moslem. He does his five daily prayers, gives alms to the poor, fasts during the month of Ramadan, and, if he has the means, makes the pilgrimage to Mecca.

The practice of the Moslem faith manifests itself everywhere, even in such profane places as the teahouses. Daily life is punctuated with the rituals spelled out in the Koran, and Ramadan is the most strictly observed of all. During this ninth month of the Islamic year, the samovars remain unlit throughout the country until that moment each day when a white thread cannot be distinguished from a black one.

Traditional Afghan society is based on a religious belief that stresses the equality of men before God—which explains its lack of a clergy. This makes it possible for people of different social classes to form close relationships. The merchant in the bazaar does not hesitate to ask about your religion. The only sin is to have none. But if you answer that you are a Christian, he gravely nods his head, slowly strokes his beard, and, with a satisfied air, announces to his neighbors: "He is one of those who believe in The Book."

If some accuse certain mullahs of fanaticism, the dervish's spirit of tolerance largely makes up for it. Islam has always sought balance in all things. The dervish—*galandat*—is the enigmatic wanderer on the trails of Afghanistan. Pure in heart, this solitary pilgrim thirsting for divine benediction tells a rosary of 99 beads, each bead representing one of God's designations. Over his homespun garment, he sometimes wears a *muraqqa,* a patchwork coat made up of 99 pieces symbolizing the world's illusions. In its westward journey to Sicily, this was the garment that became Harlequin's costume. On his head the dervish wears a tall felt hat or the familiar Arab cloth secured with a thin cord. His gourd dangling bells and trinkets, his begging bowl tied around his neck, he travels across steppes and mountains going from *ziarat* to *ziarat*—the saints' tombs. Ask the dervish where he has come from and he will raise his eyes to the sky. Ask him where he is going and he will answer: "We are going from God to God." Sometimes he will stop at a teahouse and, as a memento of his passage, scrawl on the wall the word that expresses his innermost thought: *Migozared* ("Everything passes").

Then there are the *malamati* who in their search for God have chosen the path of obloquy. The opinions of others—whether praise or blame—do not touch them. To the uninitiated, they seem like strange individuals who dress and behave oddly. But the common people are not put off. Indeed, they revere and fear the *malamati,* believing them to be carriers of *barakah*—the divine benediction. Innocents, madmen, fools, lunatics—all are *diwana* in Persian. But then, what is madness? In Islam, madness is sacred, for according to an old saying: "Only children and madmen speak the truth."

Saint Francis of Assisi has many brothers on Islamic soil: the *fuqara* ("the poor"). Their particular poverty is a spiritual attitude of total detachment that prefers the beyond to earthly things. "You must die within yourself before you can live in Him."

Putting aside the sick, the village idiots, the fake fools, there remain those ardent and avid souls who trudge the mystical path seeking the nut within the shell, the spirit within the word. These are the men who know that the essential is sincerity and purity of intention, and that only three kinds of men are wise: "The one who abandons the world before it abandons him; the one who prepares his grave before he enters it; the one who has pleased the Lord before meeting him."

Captions

1   Veiled Afghans traveling in the province of Herat.
2   Partial view of the city of Herat, seen from one of the six minarets of the Great Mosque.
3   Patrons of an open-air *samovar* (teahouse) in Herat.
4   A group of women in the court of Herat's Great Mosque.
5   *above left:* Details of ceramic inlay from the Timurid period (14th century) at the Mausoleum of Abdul Qassim in Herat. *above right and below left:* Ceramics of the Ghorid period (13th century) in Herat's Great Mosque. *below right:* Details of Timurid ceramics (15th century) in the Gazargah Sanctuary near Herat.
6   Veiled women before a door leading into the Mausoleum of Ali in Mazar-i-Sharif.
7   Women of Mazar-i-Sharif wearing the *chardi.*
8   A guard before the Mausoleum of Abdul Qassim in Herat.
9   Herati women.
10   On a hill dominating Herat, the citadel overlooks the oasis that served as the imperial capital of Tamerlane's successors in the 14th and 15th centuries.
11   An artisan making mattresses for mule saddles.
12   A young weaver playing the *dambura,* a type of two-stringed lute, in a silk-weaving workshop in Herat.
13   A teahouse decorated with naïve paintings at Zarshui near Maimana in Band-i-Turkestan.
14   These flashes of light are actually kites caught on telegraph wires in Herat.
15   A camel caravan raises a cloud of dust as it crosses the undulating steppes.
16   Shamsuddine, a camel driver, in the Nimruz desert near the Iranian border.
17   *Barkane* dunes ("marchers") in the Khaneshin region of Nimruz.
18   The ruins of Shar-i-Gholghola—"City of Lamentations"—buried by the sands of the Nimruz desert.
19   "Qala," the fortified castle of the Khan of Tsharburdjak on the banks of the Helmand River.
20   Baluch women carrying water from the Helmand River.
21   In the village of Lash-e Joveyn in Nimruz, perforated screens are laced with thorn-bushes and watered in summer. As the wind passes through, it provides a natural air-conditioning.
22   Sabera, a young Baluch in the Nimruz village of Shirabad.
23   Baluch women sing to the accompaniment of tambourines during a wedding celebration in the village of Khawabgah.
24   Ceremony involving the local barber during a Baluch wedding in Nimruz.
25   Dunes in Dasht-i-Margo ("Desert of Death") in Nimruz.
26   Ruins at Shar-i-Gholghola in the Nimruz desert.
27   An "Isfandi" dervish, moving from stall to stall in the bazaar. He is shaking a small pot containing burning isfand, seeds of wild rue believed to ward off the evil eye.
28   A tin merchant in the Tashqurghan bazaar.
29   A dealer in riding boots and other traditional footwear in the Daulatabad Balkh bazaar.
30   A barber practicing his trade outdoors during market day at the Aqcha bazaar.
31   A dealer in turbans in Balkh.
32   A blacksmith plying his trade in the covered bazaar in Tashqurghan.
33   A master blacksmith.
34   The *kebabi,* a broiled-meat vendor in Pul-i-Khumri.

1

*"Khorassan is the oyster of the world,
and Herat is its pearl"*

Persian proverb

3

4

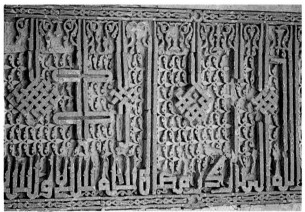

5

6

8

11

12

13

14

2

"Outside, not a leaf, and inside, not a stick of furniture :
the walls, the sky and God"

André Malraux
(The Walnut Trees of Altenburg)

16

3

"Here begins survival..."

André Velter
(The Bazaars of Kabul)

29

33

35

37

4

*"Birds and flowers
are the Afghan's two luxuries"*

René Dollot
(Afghanistan)

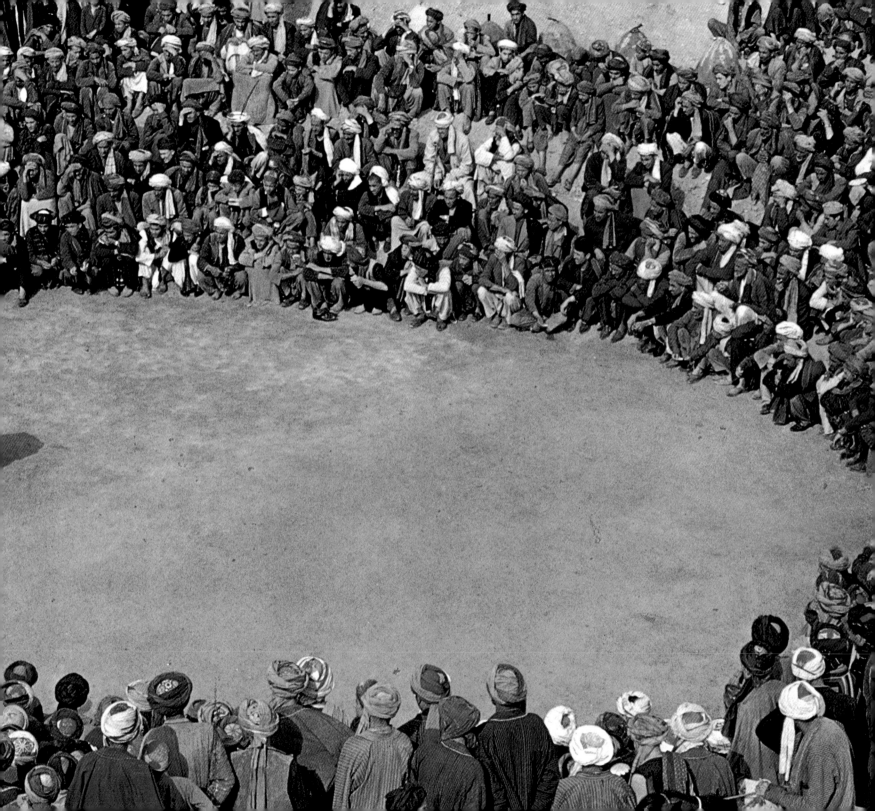

48

5

Its is said that Lei-Tzou,
head concubine of the legendary Chinese emperor Huang-Ti (221 B.C.)
got the idea "of making silk
while contemplating a caterpillar spinning"

Luce Boulnois
(The Silk Route)

52

53

54

6

"The lunar landscapes of the Hindu Kush,
as if borrowed from prehistory,
seem still to waiting for the birth of the animal world,
or perhaps to announce its end"

René Dollot
(Afghanistan)

64

7

"At my belt, my yatagan
Maintains our fame,
I am the Afghans' champion,
Khousal Khattak is my name"

Afghan song

67

69

73

8

"... in these countries of bitter cold,
where there's never a road wider than the back of your hand..."

Rudyard Kipling
(The Man Who Would Be King)

9

"If your garment is torn, your soul is not destroyed.
You are not outside the heart's deepest secret,
show your face, you are the mirror itself"

Jalaladdin Roumi
(Divan of the Sun of Tabriz)

DISCOVERED BY ACCIDENT

Roentgen discovered the rays by accident. On 8 November 1895, he was experimenting with a **cathode ray** tube that had been tightly covered with black cardboard. The room was dark and he noticed that, whenever he passed electricity through the tube, a piece of photographic paper lying nearby glowed. He concluded that invisible rays were passing from the tube through the cardboard and making the **chemical** on the paper glow.

METAL AND BONES

Roentgen investigated the rays for several weeks. He found that they could pass through most things, even a thick book. On 22 December, he passed the rays through his wife's hand. They created a shadow of the bones in her hand and her two rings, because only the bones and the metal had blocked the rays.

WHAT HAPPENED NEXT?
Roentgen published his discovery in a German scientific journal on 5 January 1896 and the news spread fast around the world. Today, X-ray machines are used by doctors and dentists everywhere to examine bones and teeth.

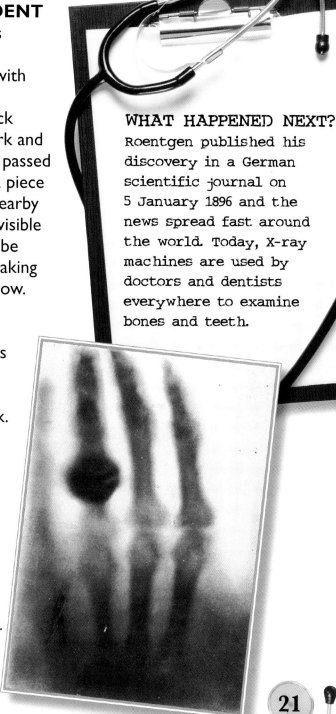

The first X-ray ever shows ▶ Roentgen's wife's hand.

21

Wonder Drug
Discovered

Felix Hoffmann

1899

A wonderful new medicine has just been launched. It is called Aspirin and it relieves severe aches and pains!

SURPRISE DISCOVERY

The drug was made by Felix Hoffmann, a German chemist. He added a group of chemicals called acetyl to salicylic acid. Salicylic acid is known to reduce pain, but Hoffman was surprised to find that the new medicine reduces swelling, too. It also lowers the high temperature of patients with **fever** Hoffman's father is one person who will benefit from the new medicine. He suffers severe pain due to **rheumatism**.

Powdered Aspirin is now available in bottles! ▶

CENTURIES-OLD REMEDY

Some plants contain natural salicin. For centuries they have been ground up and taken to relieve pain. However, salicin irritates the stomach and so the pure acid is only given to people who, like Hoffman's father, are in extreme pain.

▲ Laudanum is now available for babies too!

LAUDANUM – BAD IDEA

Laudanum is a form of opium and is now illegal (against the law). Before Aspirin, however, many people took laudanum to deaden toothache and other pains. Mothers even gave it to babies to stop them crying when they were teething.

WHAT HAPPENED NEXT?

Aspirin was first sold as a powder in a bottle, but was later made as pills. It is one of the most famous medicines of all time. Today, however, doctors are concerned that Aspirin is not safe for children, and so they are given other painkillers.

23

Miracle Cure

1945

The Nobel Prize for Medicine has been awarded to these three great scientists – Alexander Fleming, Howard Florey, and Ernst Chain – for the discovery and development of **penicillin**.

▲ Fleming, Florey, and Chain being presented with the Nobel Prize for Medicine.

BACTERIA KILLER

"When I woke up on 28 September 1928," said Alexander Fleming, "I certainly didn't plan to revolutionize medicine by discovering the world's first antibiotic, or bacteria killer." But that is exactly what he did.

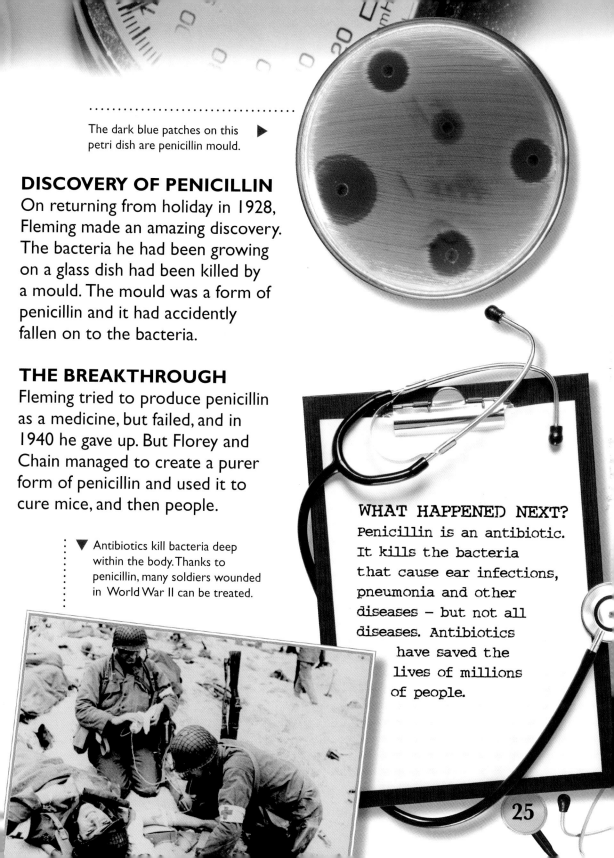

The dark blue patches on this petri dish are penicillin mould. ▶

DISCOVERY OF PENICILLIN

On returning from holiday in 1928, Fleming made an amazing discovery. The bacteria he had been growing on a glass dish had been killed by a mould. The mould was a form of penicillin and it had accidently fallen on to the bacteria.

THE BREAKTHROUGH

Fleming tried to produce penicillin as a medicine, but failed, and in 1940 he gave up. But Florey and Chain managed to create a purer form of penicillin and used it to cure mice, and then people.

▼ Antibiotics kill bacteria deep within the body. Thanks to penicillin, many soldiers wounded in World War II can be treated.

WHAT HAPPENED NEXT?
Penicillin is an antibiotic. It kills the bacteria that cause ear infections, pneumonia and other diseases – but not all diseases. Antibiotics have saved the lives of millions of people.

25

MRI Scanner Sees Everything

An amazing new machine, called an **MRI** scanner, will allow doctors to see everything inside the body. Unlike an **X-ray**, which shows only hard bones, an **MRI** scan shows all the soft parts as well. It even shows cancer tumours.

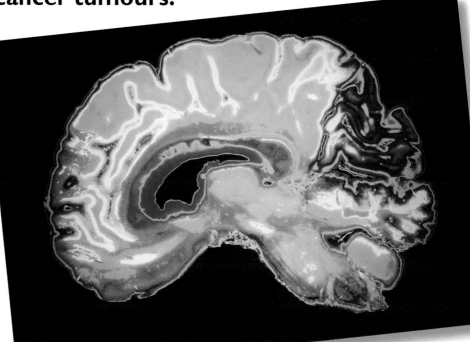

▼ An MRI scan of a person's brain

26

INDOMITABLE

American doctor Raymond Damadian has created a machine that can scan humans for diseases such as cancer. In 1970, Damadian first noticed that a machine that combines **radio waves** and **magnetism** could detect cancer tumours in rats. Other scientists did not think it would work, but Damadian has spent the last seven years building his own scanner. He calls it *Indomitable*.

▲ Damadian explains how his MRI scanner works.

THE FIRST SCAN

On 3 July 1977 Damadian and his team carried out the first human body scan. It took 4 hours and 45 minutes, but it produced a clear picture of the heart, lungs, and chest. It has convinced his colleagues that the machine will work.

STRANGE EXPERIENCE

Having a scan can feel strange. The patient lies on a table, which then moves into the scanner's narrow tunnel. The tunnel is hot and the machine is very noisy. Some scans take 30 to 40 minutes, but others are done in seconds.

WHAT HAPPENED NEXT?

MRI scanners now work faster and have been used in hospitals around the world since the 1980s. They are used to diagnose many kinds of problems from strained muscles to tumours in the brain.

27

New Hearts in the Future

Today

In France, Professor Alain Carpentier has invented an artificial heart. "I couldn't stand seeing young, active people aged 40 dying from massive heart attacks," he said. He has spent nearly 20 years developing the artificial heart, and expects it to be ready to use in patients by 2011.

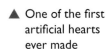

▲ One of the first artificial hearts ever made

NEW HEARTS NEEDED

Heart failure kills up to 17 million people worldwide every year. These people desperately need new hearts. Different groups of scientists are working hard to produce entirely new hearts.

28

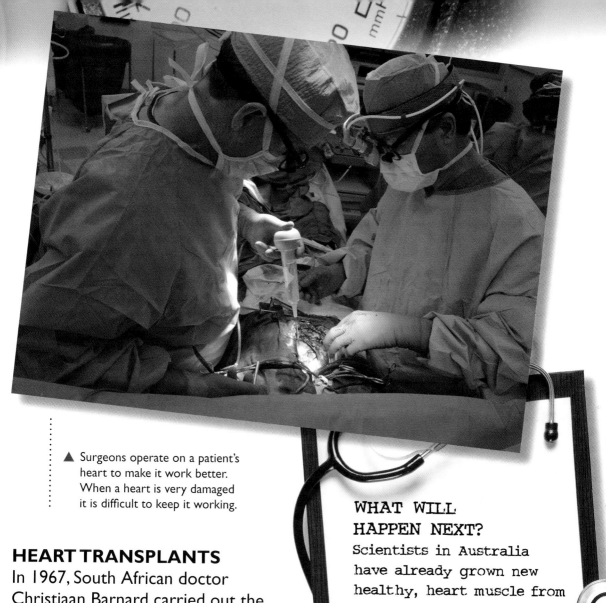

▲ Surgeons operate on a patient's
heart to make it work better.
When a heart is very damaged
it is difficult to keep it working.

HEART TRANSPLANTS
In 1967, South African doctor
Christiaan Barnard carried out the
first successful **heart transplant**
on patient Louis Washkansky. Since
then, heart transplants have become
common, but there are not enough
hearts for everyone who needs
them. This is why scientists are
developing other solutions.

WHAT WILL
HAPPEN NEXT?
Scientists in Australia
have already grown new
healthy, heart muscle from
a small piece of existing
heart muscle. Meanwhile
scientists in the United
States have grown new
skin and new bone, using
existing skin and bone.

Glossary

annihilation complete destruction

antiseptic substance that kills germs

arteries tubes that carry blood away from the heart

bored made a hole

cancer disease in which cells in the body grow out of control

cathode ray stream of electrically charged particles

cells smallest building blocks of living things

chemical powerful substance found in both natural and man-made things

diagnose to identify a disease

emperors men who rule an empire

fever very high body temperature

germs tiny living things that can cause disease

gladiators people who fought in public arenas during Roman times

heart transplant to transfer a living heart from one body to another

infection disease caused by germs

inoculation making a person able to resist a disease by infecting them with mild or dead germs

magnetism forces of attraction and repulsion made by magnets

opium powerful drug

penicillin drug made from a mould that can kill bacteria

pock marks scars left on the skin after blisters have healed

radio waves form of energy produced by combining electricity and magnetism

ray beam of energy

rheumatism painful disease that affects the joints

tumour growth or swelling

unconscious not aware of what is happening

vaccinated to be given a vaccine in order to protect against disease

veins tubes that carry blood back to the heart

Further Information

WEBSITES
Find out more about Edward Jenner and the part he played
in the history of smallpox at:
www.bbc.co.uk/history/british/empire_seapower/smallpox_01.shtml

Find out how William Morton brought anaesthetics to surgery at:
neurosurgery.mgh.harvard.edu/History/gift.htm

Learn how Louis Pasteur struggled to get his discovery accepted
by other scientists at:
www.historylearningsite.co.uk/louis_pasteur.htm

Discover the full story of how Joseph Lister used carbolic acid to kill
germs and make surgery safer at:
**www.surgical-tutor.org.uk/default-home.htm?surgeons/lister.
htm~right**

BOOKS
Graphic Discoveries Medical Breakthroughs by Gary Jeffrey.
Franklin Watts (2009).

The 10 Most Significant Medical Breakthroughs by Denis Carr.
Franklin Watts (2008).

Index